This Bible Plan Belongs To:

Jackson Smith

Date Started: 2020 8/14

Date Finished:

For the word of God is living and active, sharper than any two-edged sword, piercing to the division of soul and of spirit, of joints and of marrow, and discerning the thoughts and intentions of the heart.

Hebrews 4:12

The unfolding of your words gives light; it imparts understanding to the simple.

Psalm 119:130

Thank you for purchasing this Bible Study Plan for Kids! It is my deep desire that this journal and guide will be used to grow your children in the fear and admonition of the LORD and grow them in righteousness.

Choose your own translation of the Bible and have your child read the daily Scripture and answer the questions. You may be wondering why I chose to only have two questions posed throughout the study? First of all, to write what the Scripture reading is about in their own words is helpful for memory retention. Second of all, it is very important for children to understand that every passage in the Bible tells us something about God, His character, and how we are to come to Him as sinners. Everything points to Christ. Help your children understand this as they work through this guide alongside you.

This is just a very general *survey* of the Bible, designed to help your child become familiar with the major passages. After your child completes this once (or twice or three times!) he or she may be ready for their own adult reading plan through the Bible in its entirety.

Grace and peace to you and yours!

-Hilary-

Blessed be the God and Father of our Lord Jesus Christ! According to his great mercy, he has caused us to be born again to a living hope through the resurrection of Jesus Christ from the dead, to an inheritance that is imperishable, undefiled, and unfading, kept in heaven for you, who by God's power are being guarded through faith for a salvation ready to be revealed in the last time.

1 Peter 1:3-5

OLD TESTAMENT

☐ Read Genesis 1:1-31

The Beginning

What is this Scripture about?

Creation in six days.

What does this Scripture teach you about God?

He is powerful

☐ Read Genesis 2:1-10; 15-25

Garden of Eden

What is this Scripture about?

Resting, naming, Woman

What does this Scripture teach you about God?

To leave my house for a wife.

☐ Read Genesis 3:1-24

The Serpent

What is this Scripture about?

The first sin.

What does this Scripture teach you about God?

That he is serious.

☐ Read Genesis 4:1-16

Cain and Abel

What is this Scripture about?

Murder.

What does this Scripture teach you about God?

He knows all.

☐ Read Genesis 6

Noah

What is this Scripture about?

Preperation for the flood.

What does this Scripture teach you about God?

He His powerful.

☐ Read Genesis 7

Ark, Animals, and Flood

What is this Scripture about?

The flood and descruction

What does this Scripture teach you about God?

He was the power to destroy

☐ Read Genesis 8

The Raven and Dove

What is this Scripture about?

The end of the flood and the covenant with men.

What does this Scripture teach you about God?

That He keeps His promises.

☐ Read Genesis 9:1-17

God's Covenant With Noah

What is this Scripture about?

The covenant with Noah and every creature.

What does this Scripture teach you about God?

He will remember His promises.

☐ Read Genesis 11:1-9

Tower of Babel

What is this Scripture about?

The tower of babel and the many languages.

What does this Scripture teach you about God?

He has the power to change the tongue.

☐ Read Genesis 12:1-9

Abram

What is this Scripture about?

Abram traveling to the tower of Babel.

What does this Scripture teach you about God?

That his will, will be done.

☐ Read Genesis 11:1-9

Tower of Babel

What is this Scripture about?

The tower of Babel.

What does this Scripture teach you about God?

If he wanted us to be in heaven with Him then He would have done so.

☐ Read Genesis 12:10-20

Journey to Egypt

What is this Scripture about?

Abram and his wife, Saria, and how he lies that she is his sister.

What does this Scripture teach you about God?

Don't put up with lying

☐ Read Genesis 13:1-18

Abram and Lot

What is this Scripture about?

The promised land.

What does this Scripture teach you about God?

That he made a promise.

● ●

☐ Read Genesis 14:17-24

Melchizedek

What is this Scripture about?

Abram being blessed.

What does this Scripture teach you about God?

☐ Read Genesis 15:1-18

Promise to Abram

What is this Scripture about?

Abram and him getting his promise for a Offspring.

What does this Scripture teach you about God?

That he made a Convenent with Abram. How his decendents were the number of the stars. He chose the number three for the four legged animals.

● ●

☐ Read Genesis 16:1-16

Sarai and Hagar

What is this Scripture about?

Hagar and the angle talking to her.

What does this Scripture teach you about God?

He keeps his promises.

☐ Read Genesis 17:1-14 God's Covenant With Abram

What is this Scripture about?

Circumcision.

What does this Scripture teach you about God?

He wants men to be circumcized and that is His convenent with us.

● ●

☐ Read Genesis 17:15-27 New Names

What is this Scripture about?

The promise of Issac. And everyone getting circumcision.

What does this Scripture teach you about God?

He wants kids.

☐ Read Genesis 18:1-15

The Three Visitors

What is this Scripture about?

Sarah and Abrahamam getting the news about having a Son.

What does this Scripture teach you about God?

That nothing is to hard for the LORD.

● ●

☐ Read Genesis 18:16-33

Sodom and Gomorrah

***Get permission from a parent first!**

What is this Scripture about?

Abraham convincing God to not destroy the City.

What does this Scripture teach you about God?

He listens to us.

☐ Read Genesis 19:1-7; 9-29

Pillar of Salt

What is this Scripture about?

God destroying Sodom.

What does this Scripture teach you about God?

That He is powerful..

☐ Read Genesis 21:1-21

The Birth of Isaac
Hagar and Ishmael

What is this Scripture about?

Isaac being born, and Abraham sending away Hagar, and God saving them both with a well.

What does this Scripture teach you about God?

He makes many Nations.

☐ Read Genesis 24:10-28

Watering the Camels

What is this Scripture about?

Rebekah giving water to Issac and his camels.

What does this Scripture teach you about God?

That he has steadfast love.

● ●

☐ Read Genesis 24:29-67

Rebecca's Family and Journey

What is this Scripture about?

Abraham's servant finding Issac a wife.

What does this Scripture teach you about God?

He work's in strange ways.

☐ Read Genesis 25:19-34

Birthright for Soup

What is this Scripture about?

Esua giving up his birthright for soup.

What does this Scripture teach you about God?

If you trust in Him and believe in Him great things will happen.

● ●

☐ Read Genesis 27:1-29

The Stolen Blessing

What is this Scripture about?

Jacob and Rebakah decieving Issac.

What does this Scripture teach you about God?

☐ Read Genesis 29:1-14

Rachel at the Well

What is this Scripture about?

Jacob finding his uncle and cousin.

What does this Scripture teach you about God?

He bring's everyone together.

● ●

☐ Read Genesis 29:15-35

The Other Sister

What is this Scripture about?

Jacob doing seven year's of work for Laban to marry his youngiest daughter, Rachel. Instead Laban gives him a different daughter and has to work another 7 year's. Then the different daughter, Leah, has 4 Children.

What does this Scripture teach you about God?

He help's the afflicted.

☐ Read Genesis 30:1-13; 17-21

More Wives

What is this Scripture about?

Lot's of babies!!

What does this Scripture teach you about God?

that He listen's.

● ●

☐ Read Genesis 30:22-32, 43

Rachel's Baby

What is this Scripture about?

Rachel having a son, Jacob getting paid from Laban.

What does this Scripture teach you about God?

That he blessed Jacob.

☐ Read Genesis 32:3-7, 11; 33:1-12 The Brothers

What is this Scripture about?

Jacob fearing an attack from his brother Esua.

What does this Scripture teach you about God?

That he gives blessing's

☐ Read Genesis 35:1-7, 10-15 An Altar

What is this Scripture about?

The Altar, Jacob's name being Changed to ~~[illegible]~~ Isreal, and Isreal being blessed with nation's are offspring's.

What does this Scripture teach you about God?

He blesses people.

☐ Read Genesis 37:1-36

Coat of Many Colors

What is this Scripture about?

What does this Scripture teach you about God?

☐ Read Genesis 39:1-9, 13-23

Joseph in Egypt

What is this Scripture about?

What does this Scripture teach you about God?

☐ Read Genesis 40:1-23

Interpreter of Dreams

What is this Scripture about?

____

____

____

What does this Scripture teach you about God?

____

____

____

● ●

☐ Read Genesis 41:1-13

Pharaoh's Dreams

What is this Scripture about?

____

____

____

What does this Scripture teach you about God?

____

____

____

☐ Read Genesis 41:14-16; 25-45

Joseph's Interpretation

What is this Scripture about?

What does this Scripture teach you about God?

☐ Read Genesis 42:1-38

Famine

What is this Scripture about?

What does this Scripture teach you about God?

☐ Read Genesis 43:1-34 Brothers Return to Egypt

What is this Scripture about?

What does this Scripture teach you about God?

☐ Read Genesis 44:1-34 The Silver Cup

What is this Scripture about?

What does this Scripture teach you about God?

☐ Read Genesis 45:1-28 — The Lost Brother

What is this Scripture about?

____

____

____

What does this Scripture teach you about God?

____

____

____

● ●

☐ Read Genesis 46:1-7; 28-34 — Moving to Egypt

What is this Scripture about?

____

____

____

What does this Scripture teach you about God?

____

____

____

☐ Read Genesis 47:1-13; 20-31

Land of Goshen

What is this Scripture about?

____

____

____

What does this Scripture teach you about God?

____

____

____

● ●

☐ Read Genesis 48:1-22

Joseph's Sons

What is this Scripture about?

____

____

____

What does this Scripture teach you about God?

____

____

____

☐ Read Genesis 49

Jacob Blesses His Sons

What is this Scripture about?

What does this Scripture teach you about God?

☐ Read Genesis 50

Joseph's End

What is this Scripture about?

What does this Scripture teach you about God?

☐ Read Exodus 1

The Israelites Oppressed

What is this Scripture about?

____

____

____

What does this Scripture teach you about God?

____

____

____

• •

☐ Read Exodus 2:1-10

Baby Moses

What is this Scripture about?

____

____

____

What does this Scripture teach you about God?

____

____

____

☐ Read Exodus 2:11-25 — Moses Flees Eqypt

What is this Scripture about?

What does this Scripture teach you about God?

● ●

☐ Read Exodus 3:1-22 — Burning Bush

What is this Scripture about?

What does this Scripture teach you about God?

☐ Read Exodus 4:1-17

Moses Speaks With God

What is this Scripture about?

What does this Scripture teach you about God?

☐ Read Exodus 4:18-31

Moses Returns to Egypt

What is this Scripture about?

What does this Scripture teach you about God?

☐ Read Exodus 5:1-23

God Speaks to Moses

What is this Scripture about?

What does this Scripture teach you about God?

☐ Read Exodus 7:1-25

River of Blood

What is this Scripture about?

What does this Scripture teach you about God?

☐ Read Exodus 8:1-32

Frogs, Lice, and Flies

What is this Scripture about?

What does this Scripture teach you about God?

☐ Read Exodus 9:1-21

Dead Livestock and Boils

What is this Scripture about?

What does this Scripture teach you about God?

☐ Read Exodus 9:22-35

Hail and Fire

What is this Scripture about?

____

____

____

What does this Scripture teach you about God?

____

____

____

● ●

☐ Read Exodus 10:1-20

Plague of Locusts

What is this Scripture about?

____

____

____

What does this Scripture teach you about God?

____

____

____

☐ Read Exodus 10:21-29 — Darkness Covers the Land

What is this Scripture about?

What does this Scripture teach you about God?

☐ Read Exodus 11 — Plague on the Firstborn Sons

What is this Scripture about?

What does this Scripture teach you about God?

☐ Read Exodus 12:1-30 — The First Passover

What is this Scripture about?

What does this Scripture teach you about God?

☐ Read Exodus 12:31-42 — The Exodus

What is this Scripture about?

What does this Scripture teach you about God?

☐ Read Exodus 14:5-31

Parting of the Red Sea

What is this Scripture about?

What does this Scripture teach you about God?

☐ Read Exodus 16:1-31, 35

Manna

What is this Scripture about?

What does this Scripture teach you about God?

☐ Read Exodus 20:1-17 The Ten Commandments

What is this Scripture about?

____

____

____

What does this Scripture teach you about God?

____

____

____

☐ Read Exodus 24:12-18; 31:18 Stone Tablets

What is this Scripture about?

____

____

____

What does this Scripture teach you about God?

____

____

____

☐ Read Exodus 32:1-35 The Golden Calf

What is this Scripture about?

What does this Scripture teach you about God?

☐ Read Exodus 34:1-6; 10; 27-35 New Tablets

What is this Scripture about?

What does this Scripture teach you about God?

☐ Read Numbers 10:11-13; 33-36

The Journey

What is this Scripture about?

____

____

____

What does this Scripture teach you about God?

____

____

____

● ●

☐ Read Numbers 12:1-16

Miriam and Aaron Oppose Moses

What is this Scripture about?

____

____

____

What does this Scripture teach you about God?

____

____

____

☐ Read Numbers 20:1-18

Water From a Rock

What is this Scripture about?

What does this Scripture teach you about God?

☐ Read Numbers 22:1-38

A Talking Donkey

What is this Scripture about?

What does this Scripture teach you about God?

☐ Read Numbers 27:12-23 — Joshua

What is this Scripture about?

What does this Scripture teach you about God?

☐ Read Deuteronomy 6 — Love the LORD Your God

What is this Scripture about?

What does this Scripture teach you about God?

☐ Read Deuteronomy 8

Do Not Forget the Lord

What is this Scripture about?

What does this Scripture teach you about God?

● ●

☐ Read Deuteronomy 31:1-8

Joshua to Lead After Moses

What is this Scripture about?

What does this Scripture teach you about God?

☐ Read Deuteronomy 34:1-12

Moses Dies

What is this Scripture about?

What does this Scripture teach you about God?

☐ Read Joshua 1:1-9

Joshua Leads Israel

What is this Scripture about?

What does this Scripture teach you about God?

☐ Read Joshua 2

Rahab and the Spies

What is this Scripture about?

What does this Scripture teach you about God?

☐ Read Joshua 3

Crossing the Jordan River

What is this Scripture about?

What does this Scripture teach you about God?

☐ Read Joshua 4 Crossing the Jordan River (cont.)

What is this Scripture about?

What does this Scripture teach you about God?

☐ Read Joshua 6:12-27 Fall of Jericho

What is this Scripture about?

What does this Scripture teach you about God?

☐ Read Joshua 23:1-11; 24:29

Be Courageous

What is this Scripture about?

What does this Scripture teach you about God?

☐ Read Judges 4:1-17

Deborah and Barak

What is this Scripture about?

What does this Scripture teach you about God?

☐ Read Judges 4:18-24 — The Bravery of Jael

What is this Scripture about?

____

____

____

What does this Scripture teach you about God?

____

____

____

• •

☐ Read Judges 6 — Gideon

What is this Scripture about?

____

____

____

What does this Scripture teach you about God?

____

____

____

☐ Read Judges 7:1-8; 13-22 — The Small Army

What is this Scripture about?

What does this Scripture teach you about God?

☐ Read Judges 8:22-23; 32-35 — The LORD Shall Rule

What is this Scripture about?

What does this Scripture teach you about God?

☐ Read Judges 13:1-7; 24

Samson is Born

What is this Scripture about?

What does this Scripture teach you about God?

☐ Read Judges 16

Samson and Delilah

What is this Scripture about?

What does this Scripture teach you about God?

☐ Read Ruth 1

Ruth Comes to Bethlehem

What is this Scripture about?

What does this Scripture teach you about God?

☐ Read Ruth 2

Ruth Meets Boaz

What is this Scripture about?

What does this Scripture teach you about God?

☐ Read Ruth 3

The Threshing Floor

What is this Scripture about?

What does this Scripture teach you about God?

☐ Read Ruth 4

Ruth Marries Boaz

What is this Scripture about?

What does this Scripture teach you about God?

☐ Read 1 Samuel 1:1-2; 7-28

Hannah's Son

What is this Scripture about?

What does this Scripture teach you about God?

☐ Read 1 Samuel 2:1-10

Hannah's Prayer

What is this Scripture about?

What does this Scripture teach you about God?

☐ Read 1 Samuel 2:18-21, 26

Samuel Serves God

What is this Scripture about?

What does this Scripture teach you about God?

☐ Read 1 Samuel 3:1-14

The LORD Calls Samuel

What is this Scripture about?

What does this Scripture teach you about God?

☐ Read 1 Samuel 3:15-21 — Samuel Has a Vision

What is this Scripture about?

____

____

____

What does this Scripture teach you about God?

____

____

____

● ●

☐ Read 1 Samuel 8:1-10; 18-22 — Israel Wants a King

What is this Scripture about?

____

____

____

What does this Scripture teach you about God?

____

____

____

☐ Read 1 Samuel 9:1-8; 10-14 Saul

What is this Scripture about?

What does this Scripture teach you about God?

☐ Read 1 Samuel 9:15-19; 25-27 The Seer

What is this Scripture about?

What does this Scripture teach you about God?

☐ Read 1 Samuel 10

King Saul

What is this Scripture about?

What does this Scripture teach you about God?

☐ Read 1 Samuel 14:1; 6-20; 23

Jonathan

What is this Scripture about?

What does this Scripture teach you about God?

☐ Read 1 Samuel 16:1-13

Samuel Anoints David

What is this Scripture about?

What does this Scripture teach you about God?

☐ Read 1 Samuel 16:14-23

The Harp Player

What is this Scripture about?

What does this Scripture teach you about God?

☐ Read 1 Samuel 17:1-31

David and Goliath

What is this Scripture about?

What does this Scripture teach you about God?

☐ Read 1 Samuel 17:32-58

David and Goliath (cont.)

What is this Scripture about?

What does this Scripture teach you about God?

☐ Read 1 Samuel 18:1-16

David and Jonathan

What is this Scripture about?

What does this Scripture teach you about God?

☐ Read 1 Samuel 19:1-10

David Runs Away

What is this Scripture about?

What does this Scripture teach you about God?

☐ Read 1 Samuel 20:16-42

The Signal

What is this Scripture about?

What does this Scripture teach you about God?

☐ Read 1 Samuel 23:13-29

Saul Chases David

What is this Scripture about?

What does this Scripture teach you about God?

☐ Read 1 Samuel 24:1-12; 16-22 — Meeting in a Cave

What is this Scripture about?

___

___

___

What does this Scripture teach you about God?

___

___

___

● ●

☐ Read 1 Samuel 31:1-13 — Death of King Saul

What is this Scripture about?

___

___

___

What does this Scripture teach you about God?

___

___

___

☐ Read 2 Samuel 2:1-4; 5:1-4; 9-12 King David

What is this Scripture about?

What does this Scripture teach you about God?

☐ Read 2 Samuel 11:1-17; 26-27 Bethsheba

What is this Scripture about?

What does this Scripture teach you about God?

☐ Read 2 Samuel 12:1-24

David's Hard Lesson & The Birth of Solomon

What is this Scripture about?

____

____

____

What does this Scripture teach you about God?

____

____

____

• •

☐ Read 1 Kings 1:1, 5,10-18; 20-37

Solomon Becomes King

What is this Scripture about?

____

____

____

What does this Scripture teach you about God?

____

____

____

☐ Read 1 Kings 2:1-4;10-12 King David Dies

What is this Scripture about?

What does this Scripture teach you about God?

☐ Read 1 Kings 3:1-15 The Gift of Wisdom

What is this Scripture about?

What does this Scripture teach you about God?

☐ Read 1 Kings 3:16-28

The Judgment

What is this Scripture about?

What does this Scripture teach you about God?

☐ Read 1 Kings 5

Building of the Temple

What is this Scripture about?

What does this Scripture teach you about God?

☐ Read 1 Kings 8:1-13

The Ark and the Temple

What is this Scripture about?

What does this Scripture teach you about God?

☐ Read 1 Kings 10:1-10, 13

The Queen of Sheba

What is this Scripture about?

What does this Scripture teach you about God?

☐ Read 1 Kings 11:1-13

The Downfall of Solomon

What is this Scripture about?

What does this Scripture teach you about God?

● ●

☐ Read 1 Kings 11:26-31, 34-43

Jeroboam

What is this Scripture about?

What does this Scripture teach you about God?

☐ Read 1 Kings 17

Elijah

What is this Scripture about?

What does this Scripture teach you about God?

☐ Read 1 Kings 18:1-9; 13-46

The Challenge

What is this Scripture about?

What does this Scripture teach you about God?

☐ Read 2 Kings 1

Fire From Heaven

What is this Scripture about?

____

____

____

What does this Scripture teach you about God?

____

____

____

● ●

☐ Read 2 Kings 2

Elijah Taken Up to Heaven

What is this Scripture about?

____

____

____

What does this Scripture teach you about God?

____

____

____

☐ Read 2 Kings 4:1-7

A Pot of Oil

What is this Scripture about?

What does this Scripture teach you about God?

☐ Read 2 Kings 4:8-37

Seven Sneezes

What is this Scripture about?

What does this Scripture teach you about God?

☐ Read 2 Kings 5

Naaman

What is this Scripture about?

What does this Scripture teach you about God?

☐ Read 2 Kings 17:6-23

Israel Taken Captive

What is this Scripture about?

What does this Scripture teach you about God?

☐ Read 2 Kings 24:10-20

King Nebuchadnezzar

What is this Scripture about?

____

____

____

What does this Scripture teach you about God?

____

____

____

● ●

☐ Read 2 Kings 25:8-21

Jerusalem Destroyed

What is this Scripture about?

____

____

____

What does this Scripture teach you about God?

____

____

____

☐ Read Ezra 1 King Cyrus

What is this Scripture about?

____

____

____

What does this Scripture teach you about God?

____

____

____

● ●

☐ Read Ezra 3 Rebuilding the Altar and Temple

What is this Scripture about?

____

____

____

What does this Scripture teach you about God?

____

____

____

☐ Read Ezra 6:14-22

King Darius

What is this Scripture about?

____

____

____

What does this Scripture teach you about God?

____

____

____

● ●

☐ Read Esther 1

The Queen's Refusal

What is this Scripture about?

____

____

____

What does this Scripture teach you about God?

____

____

____

☐ Read Esther 2

A New Queen

What is this Scripture about?

____

____

____

What does this Scripture teach you about God?

____

____

____

● ●

☐ Read Esther 3

The Decree

What is this Scripture about?

____

____

____

What does this Scripture teach you about God?

____

____

____

☐ Read Esther 4

Brave Esther

What is this Scripture about?

What does this Scripture teach you about God?

☐ Read Esther 5

The Gallows

What is this Scripture about?

What does this Scripture teach you about God?

☐ Read Esther 6

Haman's Shame

What is this Scripture about?

What does this Scripture teach you about God?

☐ Read Esther 7

Haman's Plot

What is this Scripture about?

What does this Scripture teach you about God?

☐ Read Esther 8

Mordecai

What is this Scripture about?

What does this Scripture teach you about God?

● ●

☐ Read Job 1

Meet Job

What is this Scripture about?

What does this Scripture teach you about God?

☐ Read Job 2

Satan Asks God to Test Job

What is this Scripture about?

What does this Scripture teach you about God?

☐ Read Job 3

Job Speaks

What is this Scripture about?

What does this Scripture teach you about God?

☐ Read Job 38

The LORD Speaks

What is this Scripture about?

What does this Scripture teach you about God?

☐ Read Job 39

The LORD Speaks (cont.)

What is this Scripture about?

What does this Scripture teach you about God?

☐ Read Job 42

The LORD Blesses Job Again

What is this Scripture about?

What does this Scripture teach you about God?

☐ Read Psalm 1

Blessed are the Righteous

What is this Scripture about?

What does this Scripture teach you about God?

☐ Read Psalm 8

How Majestic is Your Name

What is this Scripture about?

What does this Scripture teach you about God?

☐ Read Psalm 14

The Fool Says in His Heart There is No God

What is this Scripture about?

What does this Scripture teach you about God?

☐ Read Psalm 23

The LORD is My Shepherd

What is this Scripture about?

___

What does this Scripture teach you about God?

___

● ●

☐ Read Psalm 24

Who is this King of Glory?

What is this Scripture about?

___

What does this Scripture teach you about God?

___

☐ Read Psalm 66

Shout for Joy to God

What is this Scripture about?

____

____

____

What does this Scripture teach you about God?

____

____

____

● ●

☐ Read Psalm 100

Shout for Joy to the Lord All the Earth

What is this Scripture about?

____

____

____

What does this Scripture teach you about God?

____

____

____

☐ Read Psalm 103

Praise the LORD my soul

What is this Scripture about?

What does this Scripture teach you about God?

☐ Read Psalm 121

I Lift My Eyes Unto the Hills, Where Does My Help Come From?

What is this Scripture about?

What does this Scripture teach you about God?

☐ Read Psalm 127

Children are a Blessing

What is this Scripture about?

What does this Scripture teach you about God?

☐ Read Proverbs 1

Wisdom of GOD

What is this Scripture about?

What does this Scripture teach you about God?

☐ Read Proverbs 3:1-8

Trust in the LORD With All Your Heart

What is this Scripture about?

____

____

____

What does this Scripture teach you about God?

____

____

____

● ●

☐ Read Proverbs 15:1-5

Gentle Answers Turn Away Wrath

What is this Scripture about?

____

____

____

What does this Scripture teach you about God?

____

____

____

☐ Read Proverbs 30:5-6

Every Word of GOD is Flawless

What is this Scripture about?

___

___

___

What does this Scripture teach you about God?

___

___

___

• •

☐ Read Proverbs 31:10-31

A Righteous Woman

What is this Scripture about?

___

___

___

What does this Scripture teach you about God?

___

___

___

☐ Read Ecclesiastes 3:1-8

There is a Season for Everything

What is this Scripture about?

What does this Scripture teach you about God?

☐ Read Isaiah 7:14; 9:6-7

The Messiah is Foretold

What is this Scripture about?

What does this Scripture teach you about God?

☐ Read Isaiah 53

He Was Crushed For Our Transgressions

What is this Scripture about?

What does this Scripture teach you about God?

☐ Read Daniel 1:1-21

Daniel's Food

What is this Scripture about?

What does this Scripture teach you about God?

☐ Read Daniel 2:16-20,24-30, 46-49 The Dream of King Nebuchadnezzar

What is this Scripture about?

What does this Scripture teach you about God?

☐ Read Daniel 3:1-12 Nebuchadnezzar's Decree

What is this Scripture about?

What does this Scripture teach you about God?

☐ Read Daniel 3:13-30

Shadrach, Meshach, and Abednego

What is this Scripture about?

____

____

____

What does this Scripture teach you about God?

____

____

____

● ●

☐ Read Daniel 6

Daniel in the Lion's Den

What is this Scripture about?

____

____

____

What does this Scripture teach you about God?

____

____

____

☐ Read Jonah 1

Jonah Runs From God

What is this Scripture about?

What does this Scripture teach you about God?

☐ Read Jonah 2

Jonah Prays to God From Inside the Great Fish

What is this Scripture about?

What does this Scripture teach you about God?

☐ Read Jonah 3

Jonah Goes to Ninevah

What is this Scripture about?

What does this Scripture teach you about God?

☐ Read Jonah 4

Jonah Angry at the LORD's Compassion

What is this Scripture about?

What does this Scripture teach you about God?

☐ Read Zechariah 9:9; 12:10

Prophecies About the Coming Messiah

What is this Scripture about?

What does this Scripture teach you about God?

☐ Read Malachi 3:6-12

Breaking Covenant with God by Withholding Tithes

What is this Scripture about?

What does this Scripture teach you about God?

NEW TESTAMENT

☐ Read John 1:1-18

In the Beginning was the Word

What is this Scripture about?

What does this Scripture teach you about God?

☐ Read Matthew 1:1-17

Genealogy of Jesus

What is this Scripture about?

What does this Scripture teach you about God?

☐ Read Luke 1:1-25

Zechariah and Elizabeth Have a Baby

What is this Scripture about?

What does this Scripture teach you about God?

☐ Read Luke 1:26-56

An Angel Visits Mary

What is this Scripture about?

What does this Scripture teach you about God?

☐ Read Luke 1:57-80

John the Baptist is Born

What is this Scripture about?

What does this Scripture teach you about God?

☐ Read Luke 2:1-21

The Birth of Jesus Christ

What is this Scripture about?

What does this Scripture teach you about God?

☐ Read Luke 2:22-40 Jesus is Presented in the Temple

What is this Scripture about?

___

___

___

What does this Scripture teach you about God?

___

___

___

● ●

☐ Read Matthew 2:1-12 The Wise Men

What is this Scripture about?

___

___

___

What does this Scripture teach you about God?

___

___

___

☐ Read Matthew 2:13-23 Journey to Egypt

What is this Scripture about?

What does this Scripture teach you about God?

☐ Read Luke 2:41-52 Jesus Visits the Temple as a Boy

What is this Scripture about?

What does this Scripture teach you about God?

☐ Read Matthew 3:1-17

John's Ministry

What is this Scripture about?

What does this Scripture teach you about God?

☐ Read Matthew 4:1-11

Jesus is Tempted in the Wilderness

What is this Scripture about?

What does this Scripture teach you about God?

☐ Read John 2:1-12

Wedding at Cana

What is this Scripture about?

What does this Scripture teach you about God?

☐ Read John 2:13-25

Jesus is Angry in the Temple

What is this Scripture about?

What does this Scripture teach you about God?

☐ Read John 3

Nicodemus Visits Jesus

What is this Scripture about?

What does this Scripture teach you about God?

☐ Read John 3:22-36

John the Baptist Testifies About Jesus

What is this Scripture about?

What does this Scripture teach you about God?

☐ Read Matthew 14:1-12

John the Baptist Goes to Prison

What is this Scripture about?

____

____

____

What does this Scripture teach you about God?

____

____

____

• •

☐ Read John 4:1-42

Samaritan Woman at the Well

What is this Scripture about?

____

____

____

What does this Scripture teach you about God?

____

____

____

☐ Read John 4:43-54

Jesus' Mission Continues

What is this Scripture about?

____

____

____

What does this Scripture teach you about God?

____

____

____

● ●

☐ Read Luke 4:16-44

Jesus in Nazareth

What is this Scripture about?

____

____

____

What does this Scripture teach you about God?

____

____

____

☐ Read Mark 1:16-20

The Fishermen

What is this Scripture about?

What does this Scripture teach you about God?

☐ Read Luke 5:1-11

Jesus Calls Peter

What is this Scripture about?

What does this Scripture teach you about God?

☐ Read Luke 5:12-16

Jesus Heals a Leper

What is this Scripture about?

____

____

____

What does this Scripture teach you about God?

____

____

____

● ●

☐ Read Luke 6:12-16; 9:1-11

The Twelve Disciples

What is this Scripture about?

____

____

____

What does this Scripture teach you about God?

____

____

____

☐ Read Matthew 5:1-48

Sermon on the Mount

What is this Scripture about?

What does this Scripture teach you about God?

☐ Read Matthew 6:1-34

Sermon on the Mount (cont.)

What is this Scripture about?

What does this Scripture teach you about God?

☐ Read Matthew 7:24-29

Building a House

What is this Scripture about?

What does this Scripture teach you about God?

☐ Read Luke 7:1-10

The Centurion's Servant

What is this Scripture about?

What does this Scripture teach you about God?

☐ Read Matthew 8:18-27

Jesus Calms the Storm

What is this Scripture about?

What does this Scripture teach you about God?

☐ Read Matthew 8:28-34

The Swine

What is this Scripture about?

What does this Scripture teach you about God?

☐ Read Matthew 9:1-17

Miracles in Capernaum

What is this Scripture about?

What does this Scripture teach you about God?

☐ Read Matthew 9:18-26

Daughter of Jarius

What is this Scripture about?

What does this Scripture teach you about God?

☐ Read Matthew 9:27-35

More Miracles in Capernaum

What is this Scripture about?

What does this Scripture teach you about God?

☐ Read Matthew 12:1-21

The Sabbath Day

What is this Scripture about?

What does this Scripture teach you about God?

☐ Read Matthew 12:38-50

Pharisees and a Sign

What is this Scripture about?

What does this Scripture teach you about God?

● ●

☐ Read Luke 8:4-15

Parable of the Sower

What is this Scripture about?

What does this Scripture teach you about God?

☐ Read Luke 8:16-18

Parable of the Candle

What is this Scripture about?

What does this Scripture teach you about God?

☐ Read Matthew 13:24-43

Parable of the Tares

What is this Scripture about?

What does this Scripture teach you about God?

☐ Read Matthew 13:31-33

Parable of the Mustard Seed

What is this Scripture about?

What does this Scripture teach you about God?

☐ Read Matthew 13:44-52

Parables of the Treasure, Hidden Pearl, and Nets

What is this Scripture about?

What does this Scripture teach you about God?

☐ Read Matthew 13:53-58

The Carpenter's Son

What is this Scripture about?

____

____

____

What does this Scripture teach you about God?

____

____

____

☐ Read Matthew 14:13-21

Jesus Feeds the Five Thousand

What is this Scripture about?

____

____

____

What does this Scripture teach you about God?

____

____

____

☐ Read Matthew 14:22-33

Jesus Walks on Water

What is this Scripture about?

What does this Scripture teach you about God?

☐ Read Matthew 15:21-31

More Healings

What is this Scripture about?

What does this Scripture teach you about God?

☐ Read Matthew 15:32-39

Jesus Feeds the Four Thousand

What is this Scripture about?

What does this Scripture teach you about God?

☐ Read Matthew 16:1-12

Pharisees Demand a Sign

What is this Scripture about?

What does this Scripture teach you about God?

☐ Read Mark 8:22-26

A Blind Man Sees

What is this Scripture about?

What does this Scripture teach you about God?

☐ Read Mark 8:27-38

Peter's Testimony

What is this Scripture about?

What does this Scripture teach you about God?

☐ Read Mark 9:1-13 The Transfiguration

What is this Scripture about?

What does this Scripture teach you about God?

☐ Read Mark 9:14-32 The Child With Evil Spirits

What is this Scripture about?

What does this Scripture teach you about God?

☐ Read Mark 9:33-50

Greatest in the Kingdom & Forgiveness

What is this Scripture about?

____

____

____

What does this Scripture teach you about God?

____

____

____

• •

☐ Read Matthew 18:12-14

Parable of the Lost Sheep

What is this Scripture about?

____

____

____

What does this Scripture teach you about God?

____

____

____

☐ Read Luke 10:1-20

Jesus Sends Out the 72

What is this Scripture about?

What does this Scripture teach you about God?

● ●

☐ Read Luke 10:25-37

The Good Samaritan

What is this Scripture about?

What does this Scripture teach you about God?

☐ Read Luke 10:38-42

Martha and Mary

What is this Scripture about?

What does this Scripture teach you about God?

☐ Read Luke 13:10-17

Healing on the Sabbath

What is this Scripture about?

What does this Scripture teach you about God?

☐ Read Luke 16:1-8

Parable of the Unjust Manager

What is this Scripture about?

What does this Scripture teach you about God?

☐ Read Luke 16:19-31

Parable of the Rich Man

What is this Scripture about?

What does this Scripture teach you about God?

☐ Read Luke 17:11-19

The Ten Lepers

What is this Scripture about?

What does this Scripture teach you about God?

☐ Read John 10:1-18

Parable of the Good Shepherd

What is this Scripture about?

What does this Scripture teach you about God?

☐ Read Matthew 19:13-15

Let the Little Children Come

What is this Scripture about?

What does this Scripture teach you about God?

☐ Read Matthew 19:16-26

The Rich Young Ruler

What is this Scripture about?

What does this Scripture teach you about God?

☐ Read John 10:22-39

Jesus Accused of Blasphemy

What is this Scripture about?

What does this Scripture teach you about God?

☐ Read John 11:1-46

The Death and Resurrection of Lazarus

What is this Scripture about?

What does this Scripture teach you about God?

☐ Read Luke 19:1-10

Zacchaeus

What is this Scripture about?

What does this Scripture teach you about God?

☐ Read Matthew 20:30-34

The Two Blind Men

What is this Scripture about?

What does this Scripture teach you about God?

☐ Read Matthew 21:12-16

Moneychangers in the Temple

What is this Scripture about?

What does this Scripture teach you about God?

☐ Read Matthew 21:17-22

The Fig Tree

What is this Scripture about?

What does this Scripture teach you about God?

☐ Read Matthew 21:23-32

Jesus' Authority is Challenged ; Parable of the Two Sons

What is this Scripture about?

What does this Scripture teach you about God?

☐ Read Matthew 22:15-22

Give to Caesar That Which is Caesar's

What is this Scripture about?

What does this Scripture teach you about God?

☐ Read Matthew 22:34-46

The Greatest Commandment

What is this Scripture about?

____

____

____

What does this Scripture teach you about God?

____

____

____

☐ Read Mark 12:41-44

The Widow's Offering

What is this Scripture about?

____

____

____

What does this Scripture teach you about God?

____

____

____

☐ Read Matthew 24:1-51 Signs of the Second Coming

What is this Scripture about?

What does this Scripture teach you about God?

☐ Read Matthew 25:1-13 Parable of the Ten Virgins

What is this Scripture about?

What does this Scripture teach you about God?

☐ Read Matthew 25:31-46

Parable of Sheep and Goats

What is this Scripture about?

____

____

____

What does this Scripture teach you about God?

____

____

____

● ●

☐ Read Matthew 26:1-16

Plot Against Jesus

What is this Scripture about?

____

____

____

What does this Scripture teach you about God?

____

____

____

☐ Read Matthew 26:17-35 The Last Supper

What is this Scripture about?

What does this Scripture teach you about God?

☐ Read John 13:2-17 Jesus Washes the Disciples Feet

What is this Scripture about?

What does this Scripture teach you about God?

☐ Read John 14:1-31

Jesus Comforts His Disciples

What is this Scripture about?

____

What does this Scripture teach you about God?

☐ Read John 15:1-17

Love One Another

What is this Scripture about?

What does this Scripture teach you about God?

☐ Read John 17

Jesus Prays for His Followers

What is this Scripture about?

____

____

____

What does this Scripture teach you about God?

____

____

____

● ●

☐ Read Matthew 26:30-46

Gethsemane

What is this Scripture about?

____

____

____

What does this Scripture teach you about God?

____

____

____

☐ Read Matthew 26:47-75 The Betrayal

What is this Scripture about?

____

____

____

What does this Scripture teach you about God?

____

____

____

● ●

☐ Read Luke 22:63-71; 23:1-25 The Trial

What is this Scripture about?

____

____

____

What does this Scripture teach you about God?

____

____

____

☐ Read Matthew 27:27-50

The Crucifixion

What is this Scripture about?

____

____

____

What does this Scripture teach you about God?

____

____

____

● ●

☐ Read Matthew 27:54-66

The Burial

What is this Scripture about?

____

____

____

What does this Scripture teach you about God?

____

____

____

☐ Read Matthew 28:1-15 The Resurrection

What is this Scripture about?

What does this Scripture teach you about God?

● ●

☐ Read Luke 24:22-49 Jesus Appears to His Disciples

What is this Scripture about?

What does this Scripture teach you about God?

☐ Read John 20:24-31

Doubting Thomas

What is this Scripture about?

What does this Scripture teach you about God?

☐ Read John 21:1-14

Jesus and the Miracle of the Fish

What is this Scripture about?

What does this Scripture teach you about God?

☐ Read John 21:15-25

Peter is Reinstated

What is this Scripture about?

What does this Scripture teach you about God?

☐ Read Matthew 28:16-20

The Great Commission

What is this Scripture about?

What does this Scripture teach you about God?

☐ Read Acts 1:1-11

Jesus Ascends Into Heaven

What is this Scripture about?

What does this Scripture teach you about God?

● ●

☐ Read Acts 1:21-26

Matthias is the New Apostle

What is this Scripture about?

What does this Scripture teach you about God?

☐ Read Acts 2:1-8, 12-21

Day of Pentecost

What is this Scripture about?

____

____

____

What does this Scripture teach you about God?

____

____

____

● ●

☐ Read Acts 2:22-24, 38-47

Peter Testifies About Christ

What is this Scripture about?

____

____

____

What does this Scripture teach you about God?

____

____

____

☐ Read Acts 3:1-9

Peter Heals the Lame Man

What is this Scripture about?

What does this Scripture teach you about God?

☐ Read Acts 4:1-22

Peter and John Go Before Religious Leaders

What is this Scripture about?

What does this Scripture teach you about God?

☐ Read Acts 5:1-11

Ananias and Sapphira

What is this Scripture about?

What does this Scripture teach you about God?

☐ Read Acts 5:12, 16-32, 41-42

Arrested and Delivered

What is this Scripture about?

What does this Scripture teach you about God?

☐ Read Acts 6:8-15

Stephen Seized

What is this Scripture about?

What does this Scripture teach you about God?

☐ Read Acts 7:1-53

Stephen's Speech

What is this Scripture about?

What does this Scripture teach you about God?

☐ Read Acts 8:26-39

Philip and the Ethiopian Eunuch

What is this Scripture about?

What does this Scripture teach you about God?

☐ Read Acts 9:1-9

Jesus Appears to Saul

What is this Scripture about?

What does this Scripture teach you about God?

☐ Read Acts 9:10-18

Paul Gets His Sight Back

What is this Scripture about?

What does this Scripture teach you about God?

☐ Read Acts 9:32-42

Aeneas and Dorcas

What is this Scripture about?

What does this Scripture teach you about God?

☐ Read Acts 10:1-8

Angel Appears to Cornelius

What is this Scripture about?

What does this Scripture teach you about God?

☐ Read Acts 10:9-23

Gospel to the Gentiles

What is this Scripture about?

What does this Scripture teach you about God?

☐ Read Acts 10:24-48 — Peter Teaches Cornelius

What is this Scripture about?

___

___

___

What does this Scripture teach you about God?

___

___

___

● ●

☐ Read Acts 11:19-26 — Believers Are Called Christians

What is this Scripture about?

___

___

___

What does this Scripture teach you about God?

___

___

___

☐ Read Acts 12:1-11

James is Martyred & Peter is Freed From Prison

What is this Scripture about?

What does this Scripture teach you about God?

☐ Read Acts 16:9-15

Paul in Macedonia and Lydia

What is this Scripture about?

What does this Scripture teach you about God?

☐ Read Acts 16:16-34

A Jailer Converts

What is this Scripture about?

What does this Scripture teach you about God?

☐ Read Acts 17:16-33

Paul Preaches at Mars Hill

What is this Scripture about?

What does this Scripture teach you about God?

☐ Read Act 18:1-11 — Paul Teaches Gentiles

What is this Scripture about?

What does this Scripture teach you about God?

☐ Read Acts 18:24-28; 19:1-6 — Holy Spirit is Given

What is this Scripture about?

What does this Scripture teach you about God?

☐ Read Acts 20:17-38 Paul Leaves the Ephesians

What is this Scripture about?

What does this Scripture teach you about God?

● ●

☐ Read Acts 21:8-14, 26-36 Paul is Arrested

What is this Scripture about?

What does this Scripture teach you about God?

☐ Read Acts 21:37-40; 22:1-21

Paul's Testimony

What is this Scripture about?

What does this Scripture teach you about God?

☐ Read Acts 23:1-11

Paul Sees the Lord in a Vision

What is this Scripture about?

What does this Scripture teach you about God?

☐ Read Acts 23:12-35

Forty Men Plot to Kill Paul

What is this Scripture about?

____

____

____

What does this Scripture teach you about God?

____

____

____

● ●

☐ Read Acts 24:10-27

Paul Defends Himself

What is this Scripture about?

____

____

____

What does this Scripture teach you about God?

____

____

____

☐ Read Acts 26:1-32

Paul and King Agrippa

What is this Scripture about?

What does this Scripture teach you about God?

● ●

☐ Read Acts 27:1-11, 18-26, 40-44

Paul's Perilous Journey

What is this Scripture about?

What does this Scripture teach you about God?

☐ Read Acts 28:1-11

Paul is Shipwrecked on Malta

What is this Scripture about?

____

____

____

What does this Scripture teach you about God?

____

____

____

☐ Read Romans 1

God's Wrath Against Sinful Humanity

What is this Scripture about?

____

____

____

What does this Scripture teach you about God?

____

____

____

☐ Read Romans 2:1-2, 6-11

God Renders to Every Man

What is this Scripture about?

____

____

____

What does this Scripture teach you about God?

____

____

____

● ●

☐ Read Romans 4:1-3, 13, 18-25

Abraham's Faith

What is this Scripture about?

____

____

____

What does this Scripture teach you about God?

____

____

____

☐ Read Romans 5:1-11

Justification Through Faith

What is this Scripture about?

What does this Scripture teach you about God?

☐ Read Romans 6:3-11, 22-23

Baptized into Christ's Death

What is this Scripture about?

What does this Scripture teach you about God?

☐ Read Romans 8:1-6

Life and Peace

What is this Scripture about?

What does this Scripture teach you about God?

☐ Read Romans 8:14-17, 24-28, 35-39

Hope in Christ

What is this Scripture about?

What does this Scripture teach you about God?

☐ Read Romans 10:1-6, 8-13, 17 End of the Law

What is this Scripture about?

____

____

____

What does this Scripture teach you about God?

____

____

____

● ●

☐ Read Romans 12:1-21 Live as Saints

What is this Scripture about?

____

____

____

What does this Scripture teach you about God?

____

____

____

☐ Read Romans 13:8-12

Love Fulfills the Law

What is this Scripture about?

____

____

____

What does this Scripture teach you about God?

____

____

____

● ●

☐ Read Romans 14:1-19

Don't Pass Judgment on One Another

What is this Scripture about?

____

____

____

What does this Scripture teach you about God?

____

____

____

☐ Read 1 Corinthians 1:18-31

Christ Crucified is God's Power

What is this Scripture about?

____

____

____

What does this Scripture teach you about God?

____

____

____

● ●

☐ Read 1 Corinthians 2:1-16

The Holy Spirit Reveals All Things

What is this Scripture about?

____

____

____

What does this Scripture teach you about God?

____

____

____

☐ Read 1 Corinthians 3:10-23

You Are The Temple of God

What is this Scripture about?

What does this Scripture teach you about God?

☐ Read 1 Corinthians 12:1-12

Gifts of the Spirit

What is this Scripture about?

What does this Scripture teach you about God?

☐ Read 1 Corinthians 12:13-31 Body of Christ

What is this Scripture about?

What does this Scripture teach you about God?

☐ Read 1 Corinthians 13:1-13 Love Never Fails

What is this Scripture about?

What does this Scripture teach you about God?

☐ Read 1 Corinthians 15:3-29

Resurrection of the Dead

What is this Scripture about?

What does this Scripture teach you about God?

☐ Read 2 Corinthians 1:3-11

Praise to the God of Comfort

What is this Scripture about?

What does this Scripture teach you about God?

☐ Read 2 Corinthians 3:7-18

The Greater Glory of the New Covenant

What is this Scripture about?

____

____

____

What does this Scripture teach you about God?

____

____

____

● ●

☐ Read 2 Corinthians 5

A New Creation

What is this Scripture about?

____

____

____

What does this Scripture teach you about God?

____

____

____

☐ Read 2 Corinthians 6:14-18

Do Not Be Yoked With Unbelievers

What is this Scripture about?

What does this Scripture teach you about God?

☐ Read 2 Corinthians 8:9; 9:6-11

God Loves a Cheerful Giver

What is this Scripture about?

What does this Scripture teach you about God?

☐ Read 2 Corinthians 11:16-33

Paul Boasts About His Sufferings

What is this Scripture about?

____

____

____

What does this Scripture teach you about God?

____

____

____

● ●

☐ Read Galatians 5:22-26

Fruits of the Spirit

What is this Scripture about?

____

____

____

What does this Scripture teach you about God?

____

____

____

☐ Read Galatians 6:6-10 — Sowing and Reaping

What is this Scripture about?

What does this Scripture teach you about God?

☐ Read Ephesians 1:3-14 — Spiritual Blessings in Christ

What is this Scripture about?

What does this Scripture teach you about God?

☐ Read Ephesians 2:1-10 — Grace Through Faith

What is this Scripture about?

____

____

____

What does this Scripture teach you about God?

____

____

____

● ●

☐ Read Ephesians 2:19-22 — Our Chief Cornerstone

What is this Scripture about?

____

____

____

What does this Scripture teach you about God?

____

____

____

☐ Read Ephesians 6:10-20

The Armor of God

What is this Scripture about?

What does this Scripture teach you about God?

☐ Read Philippians 2:1-11

Be Humble Like Christ

What is this Scripture about?

What does this Scripture teach you about God?

☐ Read Philippians 2:12-18

Do Everything Without Complaining

What is this Scripture about?

____

____

____

What does this Scripture teach you about God?

____

____

____

● ●

☐ Read Philippians 4:4-9

Rejoice in the Lord Always

What is this Scripture about?

____

____

____

What does this Scripture teach you about God?

____

____

____

☐ Read Colossians 1:15-23 The Supremacy of Christ

What is this Scripture about?

What does this Scripture teach you about God?

☐ Read Colossians 3:1-17 Made Alive in Christ

What is this Scripture about?

What does this Scripture teach you about God?

☐ Read Colossians 3:18-25

Instructions for Christian Households

What is this Scripture about?

____

____

____

What does this Scripture teach you about God?

____

____

____

● ●

☐ Read 1 Thessalonians 4:13-5:11

The Coming of the Lord

What is this Scripture about?

____

____

____

What does this Scripture teach you about God?

____

____

____

☐ Read 1 Timothy 2

Instructions on Worship

What is this Scripture about?

What does this Scripture teach you about God?

☐ Read 2 Timothy 2:22-26

Flee the Evil Desires of Youth

What is this Scripture about?

What does this Scripture teach you about God?

☐ Read 2 Timothy 3:1-9

How It Will Be In The Last Days

What is this Scripture about?

What does this Scripture teach you about God?

☐ Read Titus 3:1-11

Saved in Order to Do Good

What is this Scripture about?

What does this Scripture teach you about God?

☐ Read Hebrews 1:5-14

Jesus is Higher Than the Angels

What is this Scripture about?

____

____

____

What does this Scripture teach you about God?

____

____

____

• •

☐ Read Hebrews 4:12-16

The Word of God; Jesus the High Priest

What is this Scripture about?

____

____

____

What does this Scripture teach you about God?

____

____

____

☐ Read Hebrews 10:19-25

Persevere in Your Faith

What is this Scripture about?

What does this Scripture teach you about God?

☐ Read Hebrews 11

Faith in Action

What is this Scripture about?

What does this Scripture teach you about God?

☐ Read Hebrews 13:1-17

Stand Firm in Your Faith

What is this Scripture about?

____

____

____

What does this Scripture teach you about God?

____

____

____

● ●

☐ Read James 1:19-27

Listening and Doing

What is this Scripture about?

____

____

____

What does this Scripture teach you about God?

____

____

____

☐ Read James 2:14-26

Faith and Good Works

What is this Scripture about?

____

____

____

What does this Scripture teach you about God?

____

____

____

● ●

☐ Read James 3:3-12

Taming the Tongue

What is this Scripture about?

____

____

____

What does this Scripture teach you about God?

____

____

____

☐ Read James 4:1-12 — Submit Yourself to God

What is this Scripture about?

What does this Scripture teach you about God?

☐ Read 1 Peter 1:3-12 — A Living Hope

What is this Scripture about?

What does this Scripture teach you about God?

☐ Read 1 Peter 3:8-18

Suffering for Doing Good

What is this Scripture about?

What does this Scripture teach you about God?

☐ Read 2 Peter 1:3-11

Confirming One's Calling and Election

What is this Scripture about?

What does this Scripture teach you about God?

☐ Read 2 Peter 3

The Day of the Lord

What is this Scripture about?

____

____

____

What does this Scripture teach you about God?

____

____

____

● ●

☐ Read 1 John 1:5-10

Light and Darkness, Sin and Forgiveness

What is this Scripture about?

____

____

____

What does this Scripture teach you about God?

____

____

____

☐ Read 1 John 2:3-11

Love and Hatred for Fellow Believers

What is this Scripture about?

What does this Scripture teach you about God?

☐ Read 1 John 3:1-10

We are Children of God; Do Not Be Led Astray

What is this Scripture about?

What does this Scripture teach you about God?

☐ Read 1 John 3:11-24

Love and Hatred

What is this Scripture about?

What does this Scripture teach you about God?

☐ Read 1 John 4:7-21

Love Comes From God; God is Love

What is this Scripture about?

What does this Scripture teach you about God?

☐ Read 1 John 5:1-5

Faith in Jesus, Son of God

What is this Scripture about?

____

____

____

What does this Scripture teach you about God?

____

____

____

☐ Read Jude

Woe to the Ungodly; A Call to Persevere

What is this Scripture about?

____

____

____

What does this Scripture teach you about God?

____

____

____

☐ Read Revelation 1:9-19

John's Vision of Christ

What is this Scripture about?

What does this Scripture teach you about God?

☐ Read Revelation 21:1-7

A New Heaven and a New Earth

What is this Scripture about?

What does this Scripture teach you about God?

☐ Read Revelation 22

**The River of Life;
Jesus is Coming Back Soon!**

What is this Scripture about?

____

____

____

What does this Scripture teach you about God?

____

____

____

Made in the USA
Middletown, DE
03 August 2020

14296096R00106